Intro to Arabic

Bela Davis

Abdo Kids Junior
is an Imprint of Abdo Kids
abdobooks.com

Abdo
INTRO TO LANGUAGE
Kids

abdobooks.com

Published by Abdo Kids, a division of ABDO, P.O. Box 398166, Minneapolis, Minnesota 55439.

Printed in the United States of America, North Mankato, Minnesota.

102024

012025

Consultant: Harriet Abdo

Photo Credits: Getty Images, Shutterstock

Production Contributors: Teddy Borth, Jennie Forsberg, Grace Hansen

Design Contributors: Candice Keimig, Colleen McLaren

Library of Congress Control Number: 2024936630

Publisher's Cataloging-in-Publication Data

Names: Davis, Bela, author.

Title: Intro to Arabic / by Bela Davis

Description: Minneapolis, Minnesota : Abdo Kids, 2025 | Series: Intro to language set 2 | Includes online resources and index.

Identifiers: ISBN 9798384902836 (lib. bdg.) | ISBN 9798384903536 (ebook) | ISBN 9798384903888 (Read-to-me ebook)

Subjects: LCSH: Informal language learning--Juvenile literature. | Language and languages--Juvenile literature. | Bilingual books--Juvenile literature. | Language acquisition--Juvenile literature.

Classification: DDC 418--dc23

Table of Contents

Arabic is spoken around the world. Let's learn some words!

Arabic	أهلاً
(sound guide)	(ah•lan)
English	welcome

Europe
Asia
Africa
Tunisia
Algeria
Libya
Egypt
Chad
Sudan
Eritrea
Djibouti
Syria
Lebanon
Palestine
Jordan
Israel
Iraq
Kuwait
Bahrain
Qatar
Saudi Arabia
United Arab Emirates
Oman
Yemen
Pakistan
N
S
E
W
Arabic is an official language

واحد
(way•heht)
one

اثنين
(ith•nayn)
two

ستة
(sit•tah)
six

سبعة
(seb•uh•ah)
seven

ثلاثة
(theh•lay•thehn)
three
أربعة
(ahr•bah•ah)
four
خمسة
(hahm•sah)
five
ثمانية
(teh•may•nee•yuh)
eight
تسعة
(tis•ah)
nine
عشرة
(ahsh•ahr•rah)
ten

احد عشر
(way•heht ahsh•ahr)

eleven

اثنا عشر
(ith•nayn ahsh•ahr)

twelve

ستة عشر
(sit•tah ahsh•ahr)

sixteen

سبعة عشر
(seb•uh•ah ahsh•ahr)

seventeen

ثلاثة عشر

(theh•lay•thehn ahsh•ahr)

thirteen

14

أربعة عشر

(ahr•bah•ahn ash•ahr)

fourteen

خمسة عشر

(hahm•sah ash•ahr)

fifteen

18

الثامنة عشر

(teh•may•nee•yuh ahsh•ahr)

eighteen

19

تسعة عشر

(tis•ah ahsh•ahr)

nineteen

20

عشرين

(aysh•ah•reen)

twenty

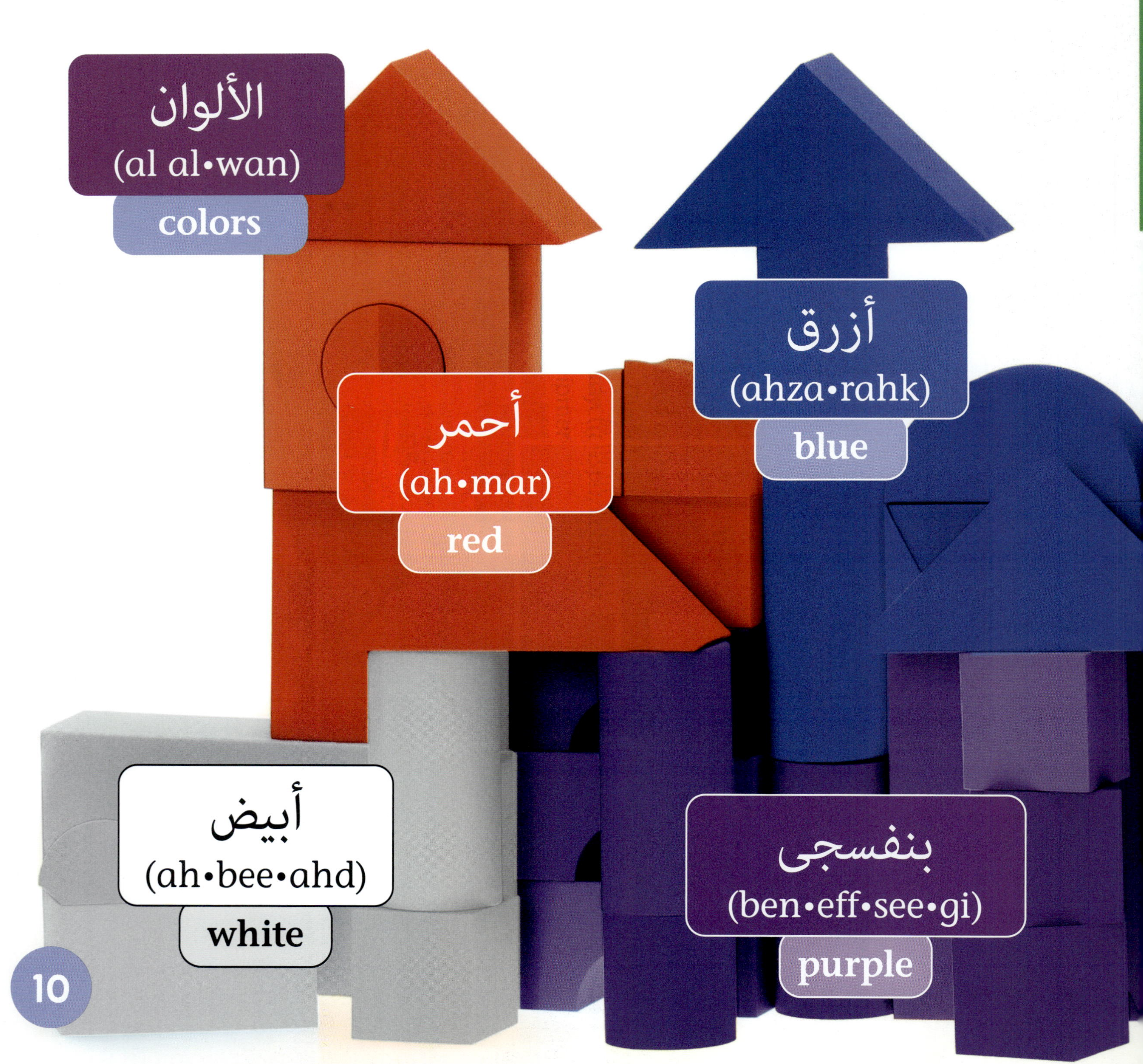
الألوان
(al al•wan)
colors
أحمر
(ah•mar)
red
أزرق
(ahza•rahk)
blue
أبيض
(ah•bee•ahd)
white
بنفسجي
(ben•eff•see•gi)
purple

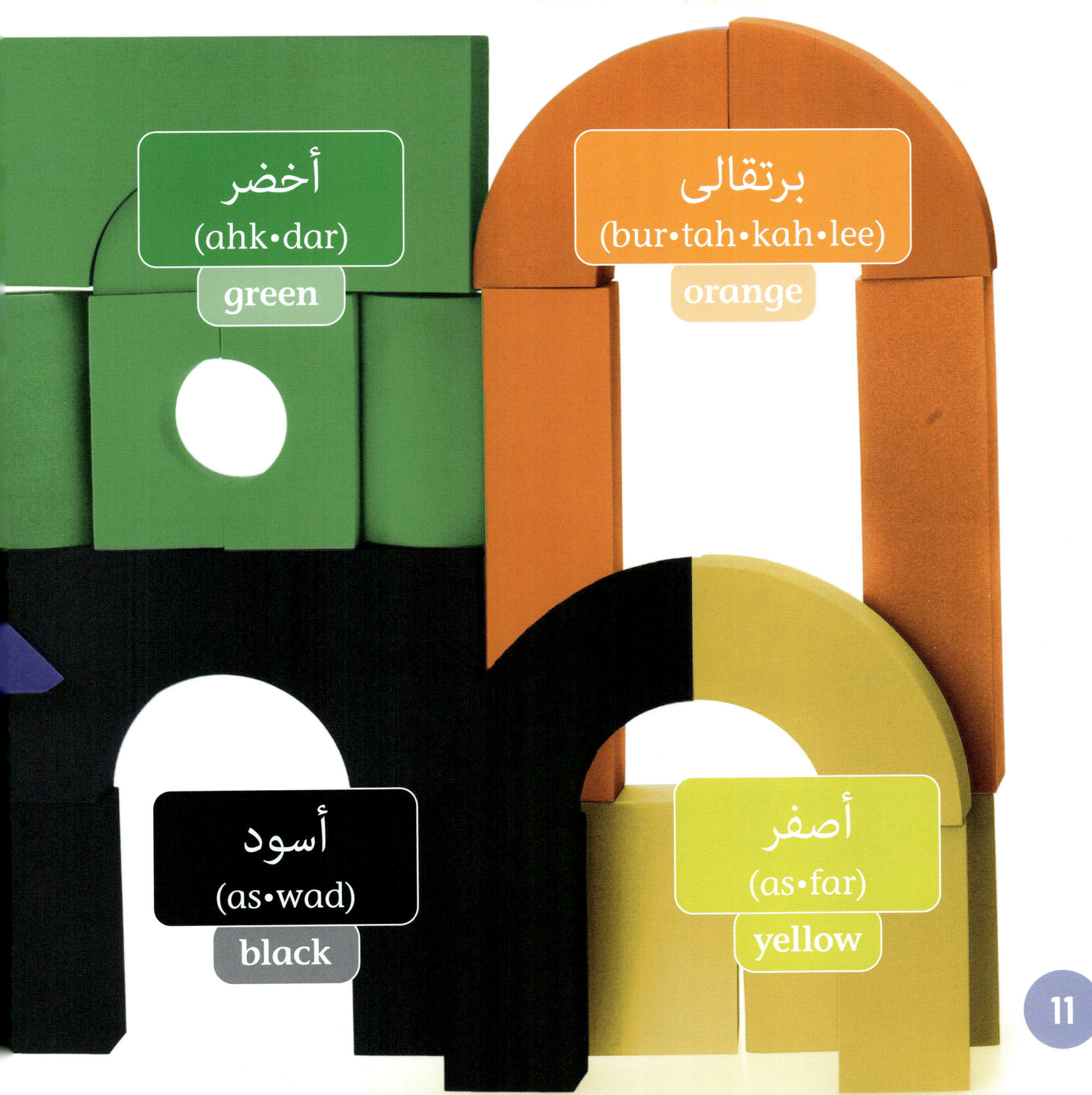
أخضر
(ahk•dar)
green
برتقالى
(bur•tah•kah•lee)
orange
أسود
(as•wad)
black
أصفر
(as•far)
yellow

مرحبا
(mar•ha•bah)

hello

صباح الخير
(sah•bah al•keh•eer)

good morning

مع السلامة
(ma ahs•sah•lama)

goodbye

تصبح على خير
(tus•bih eh•ah•la keh•eer)

good night

من فضلك
(min fahd•leek)
please

شكراً
(shu•krahn)
thank you

نعم
(nahm)
yes

لا
(la)
no

عائلة
(ah ee•lah•toon)
family

الأم
(al•umm)
mother

الأب
(al•ahb)
father

الأخت الأكبر
(al•ukt al•akbar)
older sister

الأخ الأكبر
(al•ahk al•akbar)
older brother

الأخت الأصغر
(al•ukt al•asgar)
younger sister

الأخ الأصغر
(al•ahk al•asgar)
younger brother

الجد
(al•ged)
grandpa

الجدة
(al•ged•da)
grandma

عمة
(ahm•ma)
paternal aunt

خالة
(kah•la)
maternal aunt

عم
(ahm)
paternal uncle

خال
(kahl)
maternal uncle

الحيوانات
(al•hi•ya•wa•naht)

animals

كلب
(kahlb)

dog

قطة
(kaht•tah)
cat
طائر
(ta•eer)
bird
سمكة
(sah•ma•ka)
fish

أماكن (al•ma•kan) – Places

منزل

(man•zil)

house

مدرسة

(ma•drah•sa)

school

حديقة عامة

(ha•deek•aht ee•ah•ma)

park

شاطئ

(sha•tee)

beach

Reading Arabic

Arabic is read right-to-left. Letters slightly change if they are at the beginning, middle, or end of the word.

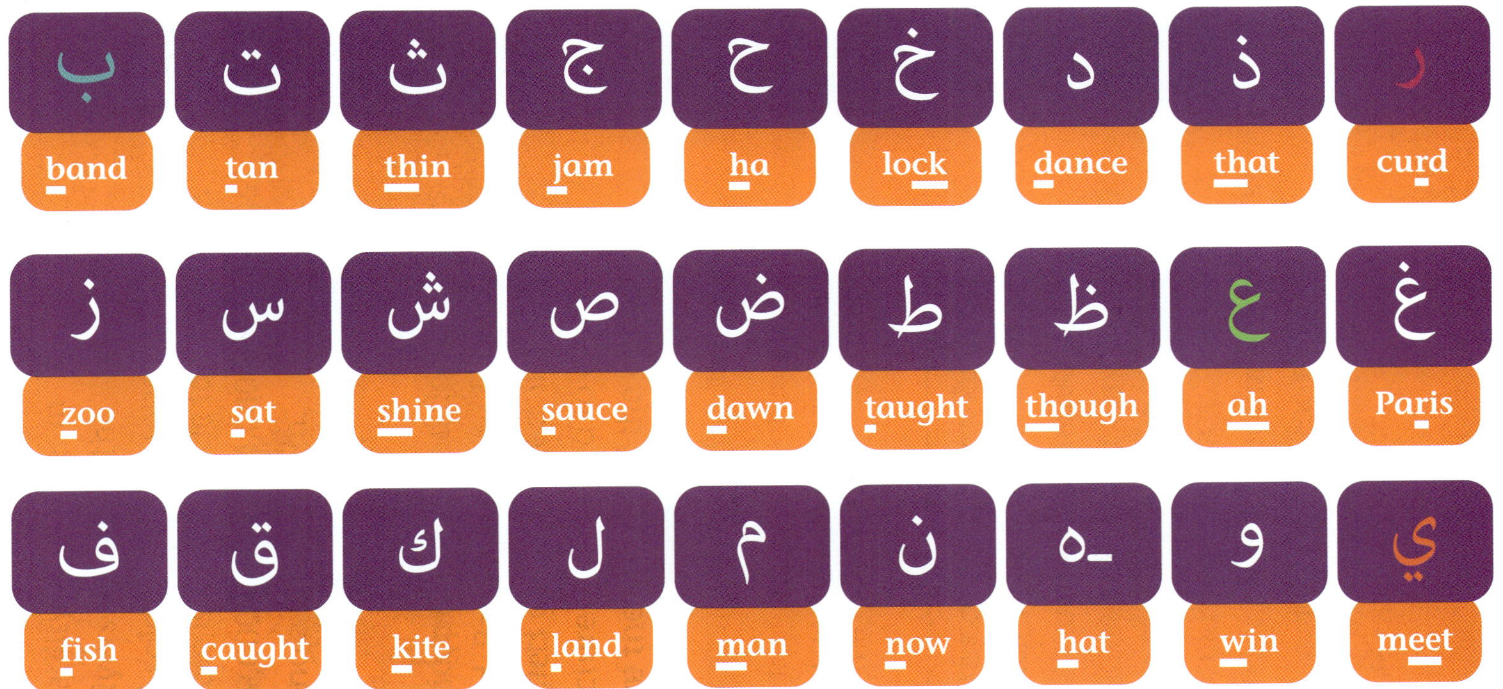

Vowels can be added to letters. Look for vowel markers to add sounds to letters.

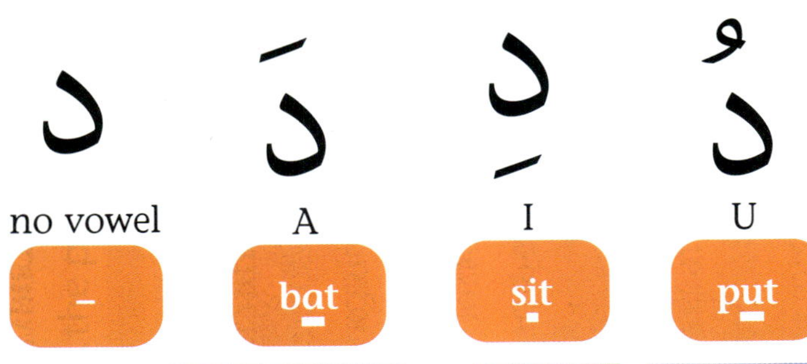

Index

Visit **abdokids.com** to access crafts, games, videos, and more!

Use Abdo Kids code

IIK2836

or scan this QR code!